by Amanda Salvary

> "The only thing worse than being blind is having sight but no vision."
> ~ HELEN KELLER

Published by Watersprings Publishing, a division of Watersprings Media House, LLC.
P.O. BOX 1284
Olive Branch, MS 38654
www.waterspringsmedia.com
Contact publisher for bulk orders and permission requests.

Copyright © 2021 by Amanda Salvary

All rights reserved. No part of this publication may be reproduced, distributed, or transmitted in any form or by any means, including photocopying, recording, or other electronic or mechanical methods, without the prior written permission of the publisher, except in the case of brief quotations embodied in critical reviews and certain other noncommercial uses permitted by copyright law.

Printed in the United States of America.

ISBN-13: 978-1-948877-73-2

Welcome to Unleashed!
An action planner like no other.

Planning anything requires vision and strategy among other things. Having a clear understanding of what you desire to achieve and a plan to get you there is only half the battle. You need to do the work, and this is where the action comes in.

To be restrained is the opposite of unleashed. The word in itself speaks volume! When you're free to dream, there's no limit to what you can achieve. Knowing that you're worth the best that life has to offer, sets you apart and sets the tone for the universe to produce on your behalf. So rather than hoping and wishing upon a star, unleash, use your gifts, plan your journey, and put your plan into action.

> "It takes as much energy to wish as it does to plan."
> ~ ELEANOR ROOSEVELT

Before the manifestation of Unleashed, I did a lot of wishing and hoping that one day some stroke of good luck would come my way and all that I ever dreamt of would somehow just "happen" for me. That was nothing but wasted time and a heap of disappointments for me.

NO PLAN, NO RESULTS!

After spending countless years attempting to make progress and getting to nowhere, I realized I was going about things the wrong way. I had no vision for my future which gave me nothing to plan for.

> **As the years drifted by and there were no accomplishments to show, I knew something had to change.**

First, I changed my mindset, then and only then was I able to focus and see life in a totally different light. Things began to make sense and eventually fall into place.

I intentionally developed this planner for the sole purpose of mindset coaching, with success being the ultimate end result. It was designed to cultivate a culture of positivity, goal setting, strategic planning, and great fulfillment.

Upon completion and thorough application, you can expect to achieve great success in whichever area of life you desire, whether it be on a personal or business level.

To achieve the full benefit of this Guided Plan of Action, it's imperative that you incorporate the strategies and key points into your everyday life. Think of it as fuel for your vehicle; if you run out of fuel your vehicle cannot move.

Included are six months of Action Planning that is designed to guide you through the process of achieving your goals. You can apply it to your personal life or for your team and business.

Ultimately, you work at your own pace, just keep in mind that it's wise to set a timeline for your achievements. You may or may not meet the target, however setting a timeline fosters discipline, and if you intend to be successful at anything discipline is a prerequisite.

Follow the monthly, weekly, and daily layout to challenge yourself and crush your goals. With six months of planning you can achieve as many goals as you desire in that timeframe.

You need to be accountable for all the work that you do. In doing so, you'll be able to track your progress and make necessary adjustments. Many factors play a part in accountability and progress.

Staying focused and not being easily distracted are two major factors. Situations beyond your control will arise; however, you cannot allow that to be the end for you. You must Rise Above it. **This is why I recommend motivation on a daily basis.**

Celebrate Your Journey!

I firmly believe that mindset is everything. When you fix your mind on achieving anything, prayer, positive affirmations, and the will power to succeed is the recipe for a great win.

Knowing that you are in charge of your destiny and it's all up to you, you inherit a sense of accountability and an unstoppable drive that will catapult you to the finish line. Guard your dreams and visions and never allow anyone who can't see them to dictate your pace.

Always remember the Law of Attraction! It will work in your favor. Be intentional about your goals and if your plan doesn't work, don't fret yourself, go back to the drawing board and formulate a new plan.

Enjoy your journey to success! Yes, have fun along the way; don't get so caught up getting there that you forget to live. Love God, love yourself and believe that you can!

As you devote yourself and make the commitment to achieve your goals, always keep in mind that you can! Never compare yourself, your success or failure to anyone else. You are a unique human being with a special gift planted on the inside. Take your time, get to know you and love you. Put God first in everything you do and allow Him to be your guide. You are Kings and Queens, you are royalty; you are worth it!

Much Love
Amanda Salvary

Identifying Your Gift

Some people spend their entire lifetime trying to figure out exactly what their gift is. Some accumulate thousands of dollars in student loans and when it's all said and done, what they invested all that time and money in has nothing to do with the gift they possess.

Your gift cannot be bought, instead you can master it. So how do you know what your gift is? It's that thing you do the best with the least amount of effort, that brings you the most joy.

My Gifts

My gifts are speaking and writing.

Speaking especially, is like second nature to me. I look forward to receiving emails requesting my presence as a guest speaker at functions. I automatically fill up with joy and excitement.

Why, because I love doing it and many lives are transformed through it. When you know what your gift is it's easy to move forward and not only be blessed but also be a blessing.

Identify Your Gifts

A man's gift makes room for him and brings him before great men.

~ PROVERBS 18:16

You may have one or more than one;
take your time to identify your gifts.

What is your vision?

_____
_____
_____
_____
_____
_____

What motto do you live by?

_____
_____
_____
_____
_____
_____
_____

Who is your greatest inspiration?

What about this person inspires you?

Affirmations

Having positive affirmations is a must.

Now faith is the substance of things hoped for, the evidence of things not seen.

~ HEBREWS 11:1

Practice at all times, regardless of your situation ABP ~ Always Be Positive!

Think about your strengths, weaknesses, and habits. Now factor in your desire to achieve. Do you really think it's worth your time yielding to negative thoughts?

As I stated, affirmations are a must. They actually go hand in hand with your faith walk. You need affirmations to keep you motivated and in a positive frame of mind. Use your weaknesses and strengths to formulate them. They should have a calming effect, in addition to being a driving force of power and ability.

For example: I am enough; I can do all things through Christ who strengthens me.

Affirmations That I Live By

I am fearfully and wonderfully made;
I am whole and lacking nothing.

·

I am directly connected to royalty;
therefore, I am Royal.

·

I am Royal and great is my portion.

·

I deserve the best and shall have
nothing less than the best.

·

My words have power, so I keep my
thoughts positive.

·

I speak life over and into my life.

·

I am blessed and favor surrounds me like a
shield.

My Affirmations
Write your personal affirmations

_____
_____
_____
_____
_____
_____
_____
_____
_____
_____
_____
_____

Pleasant words are a honeycomb,
Sweetness to the soul and healing to the bones.

~ PROVERBS 16:24 NKJV

Personal Inventory

It's imperative that you conduct an inventory on your life from time to time.

You need to know exactly what you have in stock, what you need to order, or what needs to be discontinued.

With that being said, let's put pen to paper and begin.

Note: In order to get an accurate count, you need to be completely honest with yourself. **This is your zone now; a no judgement zone.**

Goalkeeper

Setting your daily, weekly, and monthly
goals play a vital role on your journey
to success. You've come this far,
so don't stop now!

Doing the work weeds out
the weak from the strong,
the "I wish I was that lucky" from the
"it wasn't easy, but it was worth it."

You must commit to finishing strong.
If it's hard, then do it hard!

Goal Setter

Write the vision and make it plain on tablets, that he may run who reads it.

~ HABAKKUK 2:2B NKJV

When setting your goals,
it's wise to do it SMART.

S – Make it Specific
M – Make it Measurable
A – Make it Attainable
R – Make it Relevant
T – Make it Timely

> Commit to the Lord whatever you do, and he will establish your plans.
> ~ PROVERBS 16:3, NIV

Keep It Simple But Effective

Strengths

_____
_____
_____
_____
_____

Weaknesses

_____
_____
_____
_____
_____
_____

Good habits

Bad habits

Goal Setter

Short-term

_____
_____
_____
_____
_____

Long-term

_____
_____
_____
_____
_____
_____
_____

My Vision Board

Vision

So, you made the decision to begin! You kept up with important dates, you did inventory, you stated your affirmations, you set and kept your goals. You also did the work necessary for success. Now it's time to celebrate your journey. You did it!

Track your journey from beginning to end and WOW yourself some more!

Monthly Goals

Achievements
Celebrate your wins

Improvements
What will I improve on next month to ensure my goals are accomplished?

Month:

Affirmation:

Sunday	Monday	Tuesday	Wednesday	Thursday	Friday	Saturday

My Affirmations

Pleasant words are a honeycomb,
Sweetness to the soul and health to the bones.

~ PROVERBS 16:24, NKJV

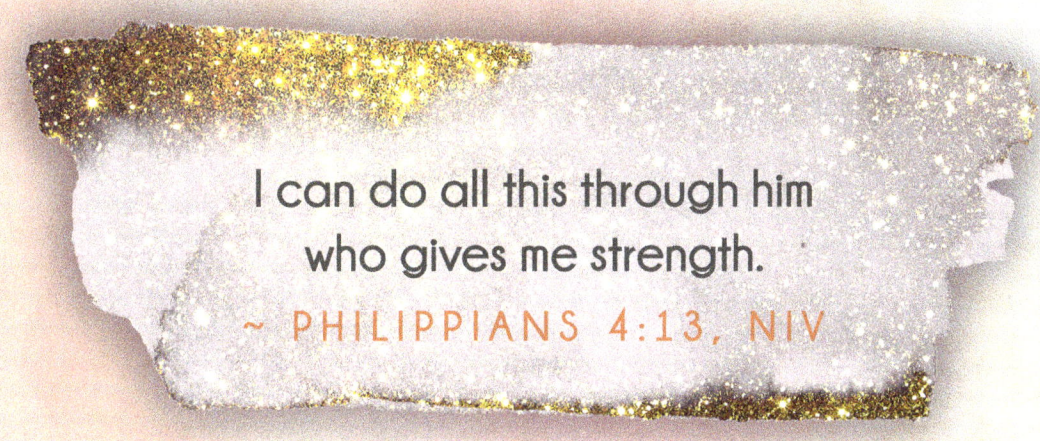

This Week's Goals

WEEK 1 __/__/__	
WEEK 2 __/__/__	
WEEK 3 __/__/__	
WEEK 4 __/__/__	
WEEK 5 __/__/__	

Notes

This Week's Achievements

WEEK 1 __/__/__	
WEEK 2 __/__/__	
WEEK 3 __/__/__	
WEEK 4 __/__/__	
WEEK 5 __/__/__	

Improvements

What will I improve on next month
to ensure my goals are accomplished?

_____

_____

_____

Vision

So, you made the decision to begin! You kept up with important dates, you did inventory, you stated your affirmations, you set and kept your goals. You also did the work necessary for success. Now it's time to celebrate your journey. You did it!

Track your journey from beginning to end and WOW yourself some more!

Monthly Goals

Achievements
Celebrate your wins

Improvements
What will I improve on next month to ensure my goals are accomplished?

Month:

Affirmation:

Sunday	Monday	Tuesday	Wednesday	Thursday	Friday	Saturday

My Affirmations

Pleasant words are a honeycomb,
Sweetness to the soul and health to the bones.

~ PROVERBS 16:24, NKJV

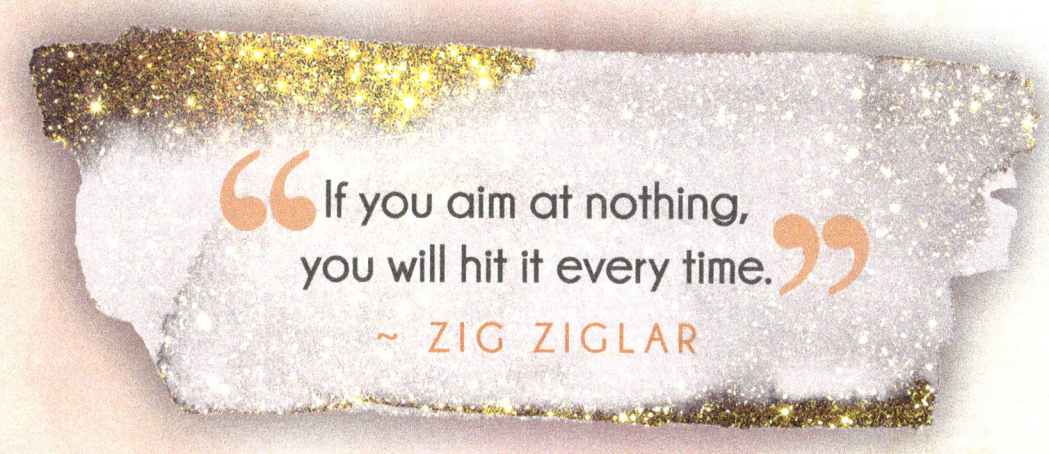

This Week's Goals

WEEK 1 ___/___/___	
WEEK 2 ___/___/___	
WEEK 3 ___/___/___	
WEEK 4 ___/___/___	
WEEK 5 ___/___/___	

Notes

This Week's Achievements

WEEK 1 ___/___/___	
WEEK 2 ___/___/___	
WEEK 3 ___/___/___	
WEEK 4 ___/___/___	
WEEK 5 ___/___/___	

Improvements

What will I improve on next month
to ensure my goals are accomplished?

_____

_____

_____

Vision

So, you made the decision to begin! You kept up with important dates, you did inventory, you stated your affirmations, you set and kept your goals. You also did the work necessary for success. Now it's time to celebrate your journey. You did it!

Track your journey from beginning to end and WOW yourself some more!

Monthly Goals

Achievements
Celebrate your wins

Improvements
What will I improve on next month to ensure my goals are accomplished?

Month:

Affirmation:

Sunday	Monday	Tuesday	Wednesday	Thursday	Friday	Saturday

My Affirmations

Pleasant words are a honeycomb,
Sweetness to the soul and health to the bones.

~ PROVERBS 16:24, NKJV

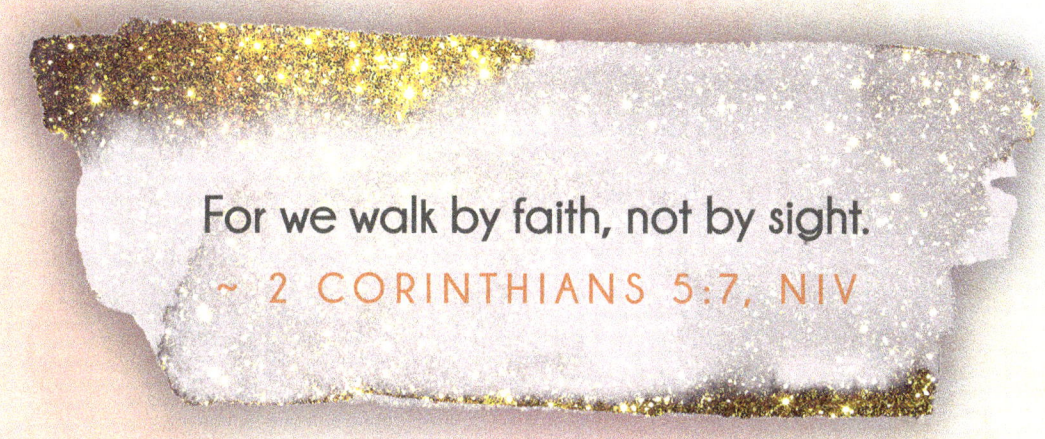

For we walk by faith, not by sight.
~ 2 CORINTHIANS 5:7, NIV

This Week's Goals

WEEK 1 __/__/__	
WEEK 2 __/__/__	
WEEK 3 __/__/__	
WEEK 4 __/__/__	
WEEK 5 __/__/__	

Notes

_____
_____
_____
_____

This Week's Achievements

WEEK 1 __/__/__	
WEEK 2 __/__/__	
WEEK 3 __/__/__	
WEEK 4 __/__/__	
WEEK 5 __/__/__	

Improvements

What will I improve on next month
to ensure my goals are accomplished?

_____

_____

_____

Vision

So, you made the decision to begin! You kept up with important dates, you did inventory, you stated your affirmations, you set and kept your goals. You also did the work necessary for success. Now it's time to celebrate your journey. You did it!

Track your journey from beginning to end and WOW yourself some more!

Monthly Goals

Achievements
Celebrate your wins

Improvements
What will I improve on next month to ensure my goals are accomplished?

Month:

Affirmation:

Sunday	Monday	Tuesday	Wednesday	Thursday	Friday	Saturday

My Affirmations

Pleasant words are a honeycomb,
Sweetness to the soul and health to the bones.

~ PROVERBS 16:24, NKJV

May he grant you according to your heart's desire, and fulfill all your plans.

~ PSALM 20:4, NKJV

This Week's Goals

WEEK 1 __/__/__	
WEEK 2 __/__/__	
WEEK 3 __/__/__	
WEEK 4 __/__/__	
WEEK 5 __/__/__	

Notes

This Week's Achievements

WEEK 1 __/__/__	
WEEK 2 __/__/__	
WEEK 3 __/__/__	
WEEK 4 __/__/__	
WEEK 5 __/__/__	

Improvements
What will I improve on next month
to ensure my goals are accomplished?

_____

_____

_____

Vision

So, you made the decision to begin! You kept up with important dates, you did inventory, you stated your affirmations, you set and kept your goals. You also did the work necessary for success. Now it's time to celebrate your journey. You did it!

Track your journey from beginning to end and WOW yourself some more!

Monthly Goals

Achievements
Celebrate your wins

Improvements
What will I improve on next month to ensure my goals are accomplished?

Month:

Affirmation:

Sunday	Monday	Tuesday	Wednesday	Thursday	Friday	Saturday

My Affirmations

Pleasant words are a honeycomb,
Sweetness to the soul and health to the bones.

~ PROVERBS 16:24, NKJV

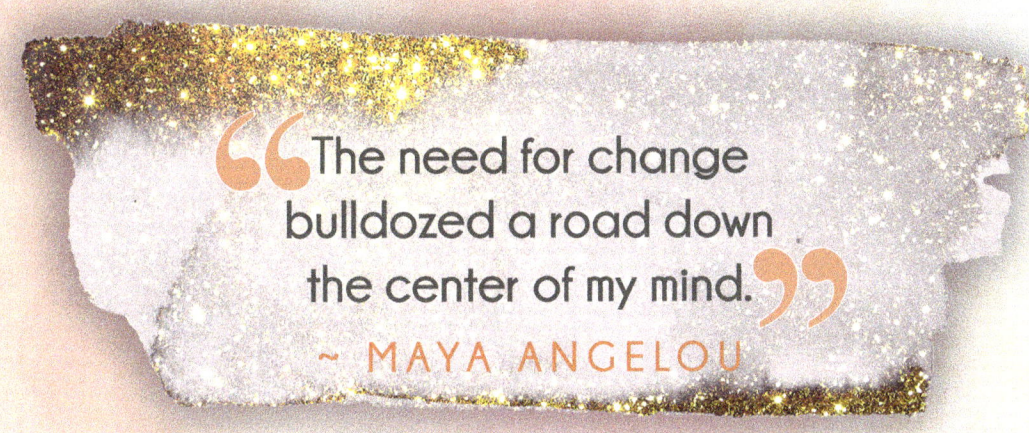

"The need for change bulldozed a road down the center of my mind."
~ MAYA ANGELOU

This Week's Goals

WEEK 1 ___/___/___	
WEEK 2 ___/___/___	
WEEK 3 ___/___/___	
WEEK 4 ___/___/___	
WEEK 5 ___/___/___	

Notes

This Week's Achievements

WEEK 1 ___/___/___	
WEEK 2 ___/___/___	
WEEK 3 ___/___/___	
WEEK 4 ___/___/___	
WEEK 5 ___/___/___	

Improvements

What will I improve on next month
to ensure my goals are accomplished?

_____

_____

_____

Vision

So, you made the decision to begin! You kept up with important dates, you did inventory, you stated your affirmations, you set and kept your goals. You also did the work necessary for success. Now it's time to celebrate your journey. You did it!

Track your journey from beginning to end and WOW yourself some more!

Monthly Goals

Achievements
Celebrate your wins

Improvements
What will I improve on next month to ensure my goals are accomplished?

Month:

Affirmation:

Sunday	Monday	Tuesday	Wednesday	Thursday	Friday	Saturday

My Affirmations

Pleasant words are a honeycomb,
Sweetness to the soul and health to the bones.

~ PROVERBS 16:24, NKJV

Delight thyself also in the Lord; and he shall give thee the desires of your heart.

~ PSALM 37:4, KJV

This Week's Goals

WEEK 1 __/__/__	
WEEK 2 __/__/__	
WEEK 3 __/__/__	
WEEK 4 __/__/__	
WEEK 5 __/__/__	

Notes

This Week's Achievements

WEEK 1 __/__/__	
WEEK 2 __/__/__	
WEEK 3 __/__/__	
WEEK 4 __/__/__	
WEEK 5 __/__/__	

Improvements
What will I improve on next month
to ensure my goals are accomplished?

_____

_____

_____

Amanda Salvary

Amanda Salvary is a powerhouse for motivation and inspiration. The Trinidadian born is the CEO of Beauty Unleashed The Premiere Salon LLC, and the name and face behind The Queen of Billions Mindset Coaching. She created this platform with the sole purpose to provide men, women and children with an Avenue to reach their highest potential and succeed. She's a dedicated mother of two and a talented Registered Licensed Cosmetologist in the state of South Carolina. Her strong biblical beliefs, faith in God and her tenacity is the driving force behind her accomplishments.

www.ingramcontent.com/pod-product-compliance
Lightning Source LLC
Chambersburg PA
CBHW041220240426
43661CB00012B/1094